Bushbury

IN OLD PHOTOGRAPHS

Bushbury

IN OLD PHOTOGRAPHS

Compiled by
ALEX CHATWIN, MARY MILLS
and ELIZABETH REES

ALAN
SUTTON

Alan Sutton Publishing Limited
Phoenix Mill · Far Thrupp · Stroud
Gloucestershire

British Library Cataloguing
in Publication Data

Mills, Mary
    Bushbury in Old Photographs
    I. Title
    942.491

ISBN 0-7509-0473-9

First published in 1993

Typeset in 9/10 Sabon
Typesetting and origination by
Alan Sutton Publishing Limited.
Printed in Great Britain by
Redwood Books, Trowbridge, Wiltshire.

Contents

Introduction

1. Around the Area   9

2. Coven   61

3. People and Events   69

4. Industry   91

5. Transport   107

6. Church and School   119

7. Shops and Services   135

8. Leisure   147

    Acknowledgements   160

Introduction

The photographs in this book were taken, in the main, in the old parish of Bushbury, which is now part of the northern suburbs of Wolverhampton. The old parish was called Bushbury with Essington, but it has been decided not to include the latter place as its history is different from that of Bushbury and it developed in a very different way, mainly due to the presence of coal. On the other hand Dunstall and Coven are included as these areas, adjacent to the west end of Bushbury parish, have to a large extent shared its history.

The name Bushbury, earlier Biscopsberie, is pre-Conquest, and may refer to a Saxon bishop. The land, on the edge of Cannock Chase, had been slowly cleared over the centuries, although even in seventeenth-century manorial papers there are many references to fields 'lately woods'. Local place-names such as Wood End and Old Fallings may refer to these clearances.

For some reason the parish developed in a very different way from adjacent parishes such as Tettenhall, Codsall and Brewood. Bushbury was never a nucleated village with most of its population living in a single community around the church. It was, rather, a collection of small settlements. Perhaps the reason for this was the evolution of seven manors: Bushbury, Moseley, Oxley, Elston, Showell (earlier Sewell or Seawall), Wobaston and Essington. Each of these manors had its own centre with a small community living around the principal house. There were also other, isolated groups of houses at places like Northicote, Rowden Lanes (where the old route to Essington crossed the present Cannock Road), Low Hill, Fordhouses, Old Fallings, Bushbury Hill and Wollery Green (roughly where the Oxley Arms stood in Bushbury Lane). Although we know the positions of all the old manor-houses we have little information on the manorial boundaries, which seem to have been complex. Northicote, for example, was part of Showell Manor.

Some parts of the parish were undoubtedly cultivated in the medieval strip system but there was also a large number of small, irregularly-shaped closes, leasowes, etc. It is impossible to identify Bushbury Great Field, for instance, named on the 1845 Tithe Map, nor was there an Enclosure Award dividing the parish into smaller areas by Parliamentary Act as happened in other places such as Essington and Coven Heath during the nineteenth century. Instead we have numerous transfers of ownership of land over 300 years or more, a much more gradual process which resulted in a landscape of small fields.

The parish was fortunate in that most of the landowning families lived locally. The one exception to this was in the mid-eighteenth century, when Bushbury Manor belonged to Edward Chandler, Bishop of Lichfield then Durham. For the most part the owners were small gentry content to live in Bushbury or nearby and involve themselves in the life of the parish. Even the wealthiest, the Goughs of Old Fallings, still maintained the Hall until 1818, in addition to Perry Hall near Birmingham.

The religious problems of the sixteenth century left Bushbury with a majority of Protestants, but also a not inconsiderable minority of Roman

Catholics. Two of the local landowning families, the Whitgreaves of Moseley Old Hall and, at first, their neighbours, the Moseleys of Moseley Hall, together with several other families like the Underhills of Northicote, remained Catholic. Happily, even through the difficult times of the Civil War and the Stuart risings of 1715 and 1745 there was apparently no violence or ill feeling between the two communities.

Most local people will know of the events of September 1651, when Thomas Whitgreave sheltered Charles II at Moseley Old Hall after the Battle of Worcester. Another royal visit had taken place in May 1645 but is not so well known. Charles I, encamped with his army at Beckbury, was offered the hospitality of Bushbury Hall by Walter Grosvenor. On the morning of Friday 21 May a Parliamentary squadron attacked a detachment of Royalist Horse, killing sixteen men and capturing twenty-six horses. This skirmish took place within two miles of the King's quarters at Bushbury Hall and he is reputed to have watched the encounter from the top of Bushbury Hill.

The beginnings of the Industrial Revolution seem to have passed Bushbury by. Some of the local landowners rebuilt their houses, such as Moseley Hall and Old Fallings Hall, early in the eighteenth century, but funds for the latter probably came from trade with the Far East rather than local investments. As the century progressed Bushbury was affected by the need for new roads to serve the industries of coal and iron in the south and pottery in the north of the county. Bills for new roads, or turnpikes, were approved in Parliament and the 1760s saw the construction and improvement of routes from Wolverhampton to Stafford and to Cannock through the parish. This decade also brought canals: the Staffordshire and Worcestershire on the western edge of the parish, and the Birmingham Canal from Aldersley through Wolverhampton.

Another development, although we do not know the exact date, was the opening of Bushbury Workhouse at Fordhouses, at the junction of Wobaston Lane and Stafford Road.

By the end of the eighteenth century small-scale industry was beginning to spread into Bushbury from Wednesfield and Wolverhampton. Cottagers worked in simple metal trades, such as filing locks and keys to supplement their income from agricultural employment, but there was no large-scale industrial development except in the coal mines of Essington.

The Napoleonic Wars brought prosperity to some of the local gentry. The Horderns, yeoman farmers of Shareshill in the 1770s, were bankers and industrial financiers by the 1820s, living in houses such as Oxley Manor and Dunstall Hall. G.T. Whitgreave built his new Regency house, Moseley Court, for his London bride between 1815 and 1820, leaving Moseley Old Hall, the home of his family for 250 years, to be let to tenant farmers.

The first sign of large-scale industrial development came in the 1830s with the construction of the Grand Junction Railway, linking Birmingham with Warrington, through the parish. The line crosses the parish from Showell in the south to Brinsford in the north, and much of its original construction is unchanged, including several single-arch, brick bridges as at Showell Road, Three Tuns Lane, Bee Lane and Springfield Lane. The road bridge in Bushbury Lane dates from the 1840s and is an 'overbridge' to accommodate the extra lines coming in from Stour Valley Junction, the 'new' line from Birmingham via Dudley Port, and the High Level station at Wolverhampton on the London and North Western system. Bushbury station, at the junction of the two lines, opened in 1851. The same decade saw the beginning of the locomotive sheds on the other side of Bushbury Lane bridge which developed into the extensive facilities including shunting yards which closed only in the 1960s.

The other main railway line, the Shrewsbury and Birmingham, dating from the 1840s, crossed the Birmingham Canal on Gorsebrook viaduct and continued via the Low Level station to Birmingham Snow Hill. This became part of the Great Western Railway, who built their locomotive construction works at Stafford Road and operated two sheds at Stafford Road and Oxley. From the middle of the nineteenth century until the 1960s and the rundown of the rail system, Bushbury was very much a 'railway suburb' of Wolverhampton, with many of its inhabitants earning their living on one or other of the railway systems. As they expanded, the Great Western tended to bring in men from other parts of their system, but the LNWR was much more a 'family' employer, with many brothers, cousins, uncles and nephews working side by side.

Towards the end of the nineteenth century large-scale engineering came to Bushbury with the opening in 1890 of the Electric Construction Corporation (later the Electric Construction Company) works at the junction of the old drive to Showell Manor and Stafford Road on land which had belonged to Gorsebrook House. This business manufactured electric rotary plant such as motors, dynamos and switchgear. After a period in the 1970s when it became part of a larger group, the plant was closed and demolished a few years ago.

Just before the First World War another factory opened on the Stafford Road at Oxley, Macfarlane and Robinson, who produced enamel holloware. This closed in 1923, and the premises were later bought by the Goodyear Tyre and Rubber Company, which has continued to prosper and now employs several thousand people. After the First World War two of Wolverhampton's motor manufacturers moved to Bushbury, Star Engineering to Showell Road and Clyno to Fourth Avenue, but neither survived the slump of the 1930s. Examples of their products can still be seen at veteran car shows.

It was during the 1920s that the most significant change came to the Bushbury landscape. From about 1925, hundreds of new houses were built on the Low Hill and Showell estates. These were council houses, but there was also considerable development of private housing at Fordhouses, Elston Hall and Fallings Park. With continued development after the Second World War, the population increased to several times what it had been in the nineteenth century, and what had been a rural Staffordshire parish in the green belt north of the industrial Black Country became a suburb of Wolverhampton.

It would appear, however, that this expansion has now, at last, been contained, with the central part of the parish from Bushbury Hill through Northicote to Moseley being declared a Conservation Area for the enjoyment of local people. There are squirrels in the churchyard and a heron has been seen on the pond at Northicote. Let us hope that something of 'Old Bushbury' will survive.

SECTION ONE
Around the Area

Oxley Bank, Stafford Road, *c*. 1905. Oxley House is behind the trees on the right.

Bushbury church. The open space to the west of the church is probably the nearest Bushbury ever came to having a village green. The raised plantation on the left is probably the grave of the sixteen Royalist soldiers killed in a skirmish in May 1645, when Charles I was staying overnight at Bushbury Hall.

Bushbury Hall around 1920. This west front of the house was built about 1730, when Bushbury Manor belonged to Edward Chandler, Bishop of Lichfield. An older part of the house still stands on the south side. Standing at the door is Mrs Shinton, wife of the farmer. He bred and trained horses at the farm during the First World War.

Bushbury Vicarage stood at the top of Sandy Lane and was demolished in the 1960s. Built in 1804/5 for the Revd John Clare, the house was altered several times in the nineteenth century. Some very popular church garden fêtes were held in the grounds in the 1930s and '40s.

Bushbury Hill Farm was built in the 1780s for Richard Phillips (1755–1833). It stood at the corner of Old Fallings Lane and the path leading over Bushbury Hill, and faced south. Richard's son, Escrike (1787–1871), was involved in bloodstock breeding and the farm was known as 'Bushbury Paddocks'. The land was mainly on the eastern flank of Bushbury Hill, where Bushbury Hill School now stands. His greatest success occurred in 1851 when his filly 'Truth' won the Cambridgeshire Stakes. His eldest son, Henry, died in 1876 aged only 36, which left a young son, Escrike Henry, born the same year. The family appear to have left the area and the farm later passed to William Hordern Clifft, who emigrated to New Zealand in 1913. Afterwards it belonged to the Jeavons family, and in the 1930s it was local headquarters for Toc H. The house was demolished in the 1940s.

Bushbury Hill in the early years of the twentieth century, looking south. The hollow in the centre of this picture and the deep quarry out of sight on the right were filled in during the 1940s and '50s with municipal waste. The outbuildings of Bushbury Hill Farm can be seen in the background on the left.

Bushbury Hill photographed around 1930, showing the main path leading over the hill from the end of Old Fallings Lane. There were many more trees in those days. Bushbury Hill Farm stood to the right of the picture.

Bushbury Hill, from the Underhill side, showing the reservoirs on top of the hill. The first, from the 1920s, is on the left.

Bushbury Hill from the west, showing the outbuildings of Bushbury Hall Farm. The church is behind the trees. Earlier in the century there were many more trees on the skyline, but most of them were vandalized in the 1940s.

An aerial view of Bushbury Cemetery and Crematorium. Northycote Farm can be seen on the left. The houses at the top are part of the Underhill estate while those at the bottom are on the edge of the Northwood Park estate.

Carisbrooke Road in 1948. The fields to the west of the parish church were part of the development in the years following the Second World War.

Houses in Elmcroft Gardens, Northwood Park. Constructed of prefabricated steel, these houses were erected in the late 1940s to the west of the parish church.

Laying sewers for the new, prefabricated houses, Wood Lane, 1948. The building behind the lorry is the pumping station, which supplied water from a borehole for locomotives at Bushbury shed. When first built, the pump was steam-driven and the cottages housed the two men who worked twelve-hour shifts to stoke the boiler. Coal was delivered from a truck standing on the 'up' main line behind the building. Presumably the men loaded the truck with the least possible delay. In later years the steam-pump was replaced by a gas-engined pump. This puffed away day and night, year after year. Beyond the cottages was 'Derby Joe's Hole', where soil had been excavated for the shunting-hump on the west side of Fordhouse Road. This was filled in in the 1960s.

Prefabricated houses in Grosvenor Crescent, 1978. Built immediately after the end of the Second World War as an emergency measure, these houses are still in use, and better than many of later construction.

Underhill Lane showing some of the new houses built after 1950. The lane was realigned at this time, Underhill Farm demolished, and the junction with Cannock Road moved from directly opposite the Pear Tree Inn.

The Dole House, Bee Lane, was built in 1832 when Bushbury Workhouse closed. As the name suggests it was used for the distribution of 'dole' to the poor and destitute in the parish.

Bushbury Lane in the 1920s. These houses were built in the 1870s–80s to house the increasing workforce of the two railway systems. Older residents will remember the lady with the bicycle, Deaconess Parker. The large signal gantry, to the left of the bridge, was a landmark for several generations.

Bushbury Lane around 1910. Children, possibly from local railway families, pose for the photographer.

Railway Terrace, Fordhouse Road, was built around 1870 by the LNW Railway Company for some of the employees at its expanding nearby shed. The houses had long gardens and most railwaymen were keen gardeners, some keeping chickens and pigs. The house in the foreground had been designed as a shop, as it was a good mile to the shops on Stafford Road.

The Railwaymen's Lodge in Bushbury Lane, between Fordhouse Road and the railway bridge, was erected by the LNW Railway Company around 1905 to provide overnight accommodation for locomotive crews working 'double home' turns to Wolverhampton. It was run by a resident cook/housekeeper and men were assured of hot water for washing, good food, and a clean bed. The Lodge was closed in the 1960s.

Stafford Road, Fordhouses, photographed in the 1930s from the end of Wobaston Lane. The trolleybus wires are in position and the shops have been extended.

Wobaston Lane photographed from Fordhouses around 1935. The houses on the left are still there, but the cottage on the right was demolished when the dual carriageway was built.

Fordhouse Mill house and pool photographed around 1933 across the mill pool, which was at a higher level than the floor of the house. Water from the Waterhead Brook flowed out of the pool to drive the water-mill, which was the last mill in the parish and closed in 1959.

Members of the Clifft family outside Fordhouse Mill Farm, which was owned by Lincoln College, Oxford. The house had been rebuilt in 1846 and was demolished around 1960, when the houses were built in Cricket Meadow.

The interior of Fordhouse Mill around 1957. One of the farmworkers, Philip Picken of Bee Lane, is supervising the machinery. Note the bevil gear.

Springfield Farm, Fordhouses, which stood on the north side of Springfield Lane, looking towards Snape's Green and the railway bridge. The young men have not been identified, but they may be part of the Moreton family.

Marsh Lane, looking west, probably in the mid-1930s before the council houses were built. This photograph shows the Three Tuns cottages.

Wobaston Manor in the style of the late eighteenth or early nineteenth century, but it is not known when or by whom it was built. The manor was farmed by the Forster family for many generations. It was sold to John Corser in 1787 and repurchased by a niece of the Forsters, Catherine Davenhill, in 1838. It was leased to the Sidney family in the mid-nineteenth century and was the home of the Petit family at the beginning of the twentieth century. Mr Frank Watson farmed here from about 1925. In the 1930s the fields were used for the annual Sunday School Treat. Children were brought in by lorry and horse-drawn farm wagon for races and games. Sandwiches and a sticky bun were provided, and tea (bring your own mug!).

Moseley Old Hall around 1860. This very early photograph shows the Old Hall before its reconstruction, when the infilling between the timbers was replaced with redbrick. The house was built around 1600 by Henry Pitt of Bushbury who bought the land in 1583 from the Codsall family. It came into the Whitgreave family through Alice, daughter of Henry Pitt, who married Thomas Whitgreave. These Whitgreaves were Roman Catholics and the house contained several hiding-places for concealing priests and religious objects. Charles II was hidden here in 1651 after the Battle of Worcester. Alice Whitgreave was still alive at this time.

Moseley Old Hall from the north, showing that little change has been made to the exterior during this century. The Whitgreave family lived at Moseley until 1821 when it was let to tenants. At one time it was a tenement which housed several families. In 1925 the Whitgreaves sold the Hall and it continued to be used as a farmhouse, although in danger from subsidence due to mining. It was bought in 1940 by Mr W. Wiggin of Bloxwich who carried out extensive repairs and covenanted the house to the National Trust. It was opened to the public in the 1960s.

Northycote Farm, a timber-framed house, was built around 1600 by the Catholic Underhill family who lived here until 1791. This side of the house, now the front, was originally the back. It was comprehensively restored by Wolverhampton Borough Council in the 1980s and, with its 80 acres of land, is now used for educational visits as well as holding open days with displays of country crafts. The Friends of Northycote Farm organize events for the public, such as bird-watching, walks and wildlife studies.

The Catholic chapel at Northicote was built in the 1820s by G.T. Whitgreave for his new residence nearby, Moseley Court. Two of the Whitgreave children who died young were buried here. The chapel was demolished in the 1920s, but its site can be identified by the rectangular lawn on the north side of the house. The photograph dates from 1913.

Westcroft Farm, a timber-framed building, was originally Werlescroft, and one of the three farms in the possession of the Underhill family along with Northycote and Underhill Farms.

Moseley Court was built between 1815 and 1821 by George Thomas Whitgreave (1787–1863), a member of the Moseley Old Hall family, for his first wife, Amelia Ann Hodges, whom he had married in 1814. The house stood about 400 yards north-east of Northycote Farm and was considerably altered during the nineteenth century. From around 1870 it was let to various families and finally sold in 1922. Following the death of the last owner, Mrs A.J. Wesson, the house was badly vandalized and demolished in the 1960s.

Moseley Hall was the home of the Moseley family, later the Hortons, lords of the manor of Moseley. The house was rebuilt in the early eighteenth century by Thomas Moseley. The front has some similarities with Old Fallings Hall, which dates from about the same time, and may have been designed by the same architect.

A timber-framed cottage at Moseley, one of the last examples of timber-framed, vernacular architecture in the parish. It stood a few yards north of Moseley Hall and was demolished around 1960.

The Devil's Elbow, Moseley, a scene that has changed little in ninety years except for the recent provision of a handrail across the bridge. The two young men also appear on the photograph of Springfield Farm (page 26).

Northicote Lane photographed from a few yards past the farm on what is now called the Bridleway. The hedgerows are little changed.

Low Hill housing estate around the mid-1930s. Guy Avenue has not yet been cut. The factory is the Britool, the large circle on the right is Old Fallings Crescent and the smaller circle on the left, Showell Circus.

Construction of the Low Hill housing estate, 1926. The layout of the estate was influenced by the principles of the garden suburb movement. The photograph below shows the wide roads and rounded corners with wide grass verges. The houses were of several different designs, some of which can also be seen on other council estates in Wolverhampton. The photograph above shows the church-type design and was probably taken in the Old Fallings Crescent area.

Sixteenth Avenue, Low Hill, which became Hammond Avenue in the mid-1930s. Originally all the streets on the estate were given numbers until many were given names with local connections suggested by Gerald Mander, a local historian. Hammond Avenue, however, was not one of the original suggestions. The single-decker Tilling Stevens bus in the distance dates the photograph to before 1930. The bus stands at the terminus of the number 26 route, which went to the Fighting Cocks via Gorsebrook Road and Chapel Ash. After 1930 double-decker Guy buses were used on this route.

Low Hill House was built around 1760 for Willis Kempson of Bilston and his wife Bridget, youngest daughter of Walter Gough of Old Fallings. It had several owners but none more enterprising than Henry Lovatt (1831–1913), civil engineer and entrepreneur. Within forty years he established a construction business engaged in all sorts of work, from railways to theatres and churches both in England and abroad. The house, photographed in 1907, stood at the top of the present Goodyear Avenue, where Whitgreave School is now, and was demolished in 1926 when the estate was built. Many people feel that Henry Lovatt's name should also have been commemorated locally.

The lodge to Low Hill House stood at the end of the drive from Bushbury Lane to the house, now Wingfoot Avenue, and was demolished when the houses were built around 1927. The lady in the picture is Mrs Spencer, née Wellman, who was the daughter of the coachman who lived in the house.

Upper Park Lane in the early twentieth century, looking towards the junction with Old Fallings Lane, before any houses were built. Park Lane was part of the old parish boundary.

Old Fallings Hall pictured in the sale catalogue in 1916, when the Hall was offered for sale by the Paget family. The Hall was built around 1720 by Walter Gough, a member of a wealthy family whose fortunes were based on the sixteenth-century wool trade. They were the richest family in Bushbury, and for generations were engaged in trade with the Orient.

The dining hall, Old Fallings Hall. John Gough, the last of the line, was born in 1780, married Jane Elizabeth Paget of Cranmore Hall in Somerset and died in 1844 leaving no direct heirs. Following Jane's death in 1848 the estate passed to her brother, John Moore Paget (1791–1866).

The chapel, Old Fallings Hall. The house was finally sold in 1925 and became St Chad's College, a Catholic boys' school until 1977, when its status changed to a mixed comprehensive school.

Old Fallings House in 1916. The house stood on the opposite side of Old Fallings Lane to the Hall. In the 1920s it was the home of Charles Owen Silvers, manager of Wolverhampton Corporation Transport. In the 1930s it was lived in by Father Woulfe.

Oxley Manor was built in 1854 by the Wolverhampton banker, Alexander Hordern, and stood on what is now Oxley Park golf course on the site of an earlier manor-house. Hordern died in 1870 and his estate passed to his late wife's brother, Henry Hill, another banker. His son, Alexander Staveley-Hill MP, JP, took an active part in parliamentary affairs and local government. He was well known and respected in Bushbury. In 1880, with his second wife, he donated the combined Anglican chapel and schoolroom in Bushbury Lane (known as the 'Concrete' school). He died in 1905. His son, Henry, was also a Member of Parliament and a Justice of the Peace. He served in the First World War as Lieutenant-Colonel of the Staffordshire Yeomanry. In 1920 the family left Bushbury, and the house was demolished in 1929.

The lodge to Oxley Manor stood on the west side of Stafford Road on the corner of Lodge Road, which had been the drive to Oxley Manor. It was demolished when this part of Stafford Road was converted to a dual carriageway.

De Grey Cottage, which still stands in Oxley Moor Road, was the home of Mr H.J. Winstone, agent to Henry Staveley-Hill of Oxley Manor. The house was named after Henry's wife, Eileen De Grey Darcy.

New Oxley House is now 437 Stafford Road and stands near the junction with Church Road. It was built in the 1780s for William Warner, founder of a family of distinguished clerics, lawyers and benefactors of Wolverhampton Grammar School. Early in the twentieth century it was the home of Henry Staveley-Hill for four years until 1905, when his father died and he moved to Oxley Manor. The house has been considerably altered and extended and is now divided into flats. All the land which belonged to the house has been sold for development, and the house is barely visible from Stafford Road. New Oxley House was thus named because it was built in the area of town then known as New Oxley. Confusingly, Oxley House was built later than New Oxley House (see opposite page).

Oxley House was probably built in the 1820s for John Henry Sparrow of the local iron-making family. It was later the home of John Shaw, another Wolverhampton industrialist, who was a founder of Wolverhampton Library and Tettenhall College and member of Queen Street Congregational chapel. By 1860 it was the home of Richard Shelton, a timber merchant. The house sank slowly into dereliction. Only in 1983, after a devastating fire, was it finally rebuilt and converted into modern flats.

Elmdon Road, Rakegate, photographed from 117 Probert Road in April 1949. The Rakegate estate was developed after the Second World War on the land of the old Rakegate Farm to the north of Oxley Moor Road.

Elmdon Road, Rakegate, in 1948. Photographed from the same place as the view opposite, but six months before, it shows how wild and uncultivated this side of the parish was before building began.

Sheldon Road, Rakegate, photographed from 100 Renton Road in September 1948. Note the rough open landscape between Oxley Moor Road and Marsh Lane before development. In the distance is the bridge over the Shropshire Union Canal.

Stafford Road in the 1930s, showing the start of the construction of the dual carriageway.

Stafford Road, Fordhouses, showing the end of Springfield Lane. The sign saying 'Hobsons Works' indicates the turning across the dual carriageway and dates the picture as post-war. Hobsons, now Lucas, was built as a shadow factory during the Second World War.

Oriel Cottage, Stafford Road, Fordhouses, was built in the early 1860s in the neo-Tudor style. It has been completely restored and now houses a prestigious office suite.

Stafford Road, Fordhouses. These old cottages stood on the north side of the corner of Stafford Road and Wobaston Lane. They were demolished around 1930.

Aerial view of Stafford Road, Fordhouses, looking south from somewhere near the present junction with the M54. There is some industrial development along the west side of the main road, including Lucas near to the centre of the photograph, but not all of the present factories in Wobaston Road have been built. The Fordhouses estate can be seen behind, with the open fields that are now the Pendeford estate to the right. The canal is clearly visible. The three chimneys of Courtauld's factory appear in the background, while the foreground, which is now covered by houses, is still fields.

Stafford Road in 1926. The bungalows in the top photograph are on the east side of the road, north of Goodyear, and were among the first developments of private housing after the First World War. The one with the gable is still identifiable as No. 344. Those below were clearly built around the same time, and stand on the opposite side of the road in an area then known as New Oxley.

Stafford Road, looking north from the end of Bushbury Lane. The houses are still there today although the scene looks very different.

Stafford Road, looking down Oxley Bank in the early years of the century. The house on the left is now The Croft.

Stafford Road around 1920, when the trams were still in operation, looking north from a position just north of Gorsebrook Road. Gorsebrook House is behind the trees on the right.

Stafford Road around 1919, showing the shops at the corner of Gorsebrook Road. The building on the right is the Bridge Inn.

Stafford Road, looking north in May 1964. The bridge carries the loop-line from Dunstall Park station whose entrance is on the right. The Northumberland Arms is visible through the bridge, with the entrance to the gasworks beyond the terrace of houses, and one of the gas-processing buildings in the background.

Stafford Road, looking north from Five Ways. This photograph dates from the early 1920s, when this area clearly contained many small shops.

Stafford Road in 1964, showing a similar view to the previous photograph. The area is relatively unchanged in that the buildings are still standing and it still contains mainly small shops. Transport changes are prominent, however, with the horse and cart replaced by the car, and the tramlines by overhead wires for trolleybuses. The Locomotive Inn stands on the corner to the left of the roundabout. On the right is Albino's garage with its kerbside pumps.

Five Ways, Stafford Road, looking in the opposite direction in 1963. The road to the left of Atkinson's public house, the Wellington, is North Road, which was still a through route into the town centre via North Street. On the right is Wiltshires, one of Wolverhampton's last pawnbrokers. The large building to the left of the public house is the Working Men's Club.

Gorsebrook House stood with its side towards the Stafford Road, on the bend opposite to Gorsebrook Road (see page 53). It is in the style of the 1770s–80s, but it is difficult to believe that it was built after the opening of the Birmingham Canal in 1772 as it ran so close. In the early nineteenth century it was the home of John Corser, a Wolverhampton solicitor, and later John Gough. At the turn of the century the house and its land were sold to the Electric Construction Company who built its works in the gardens. The house then became the home of Mr Jones, the first works manager. It was demolished in the 1980s following the closure of the works.

Dunstall Hall, according to a letter written by the Staffordshire historian, Stebbing-Shaw, to the *Gentleman's Magazine* in 1794, belonged to the Hampton family in the time of Henry II, and later to the Wightwicks. In the nineteenth century it was the home of the banker, Henry Hordern. His brother, Alexander, lived at nearby Oxley Manor. The two estates were adjoining, linked by a bridge across the Birmingham Canal. The Hall was demolished around 1915 and the Courtauld's factory built on the site.

Dunstall Hill House was built in the nineteenth century and stood to the east of Dunstall Hall. At one time it was the home of Thomas William Shaw, son of John Shaw the Wolverhampton industrialist. A lodge to the house still stands in Dunstall Lane.

The Birmingham Canal, looking east towards Stafford Road bridge. The canal was opened in 1772. In the 1840s, when the Shrewsbury and Birmingham Railway was being built, it was necessary for a skewed arch to be built in the viaduct where it crossed the canal.

Jones Road, Bushbury, was built around 1900 and was named after Thomas Jones, brickmaker and local entrepreneur. The Birmingham Canal is on the left.

The Birmingham Canal, photographed in 1975 from under Stafford Road bridge, looking west. Number 16 lock and the GWR viaduct are in the distance. The cottage on the right-hand side has now gone.

Stafford Road and the Electric Construction Company photographed in the 1960s. The car on the left is in Gorsebrook Road approaching Stafford Road. It is a good record of the time when some of the clearance of old property had taken place, but many of the old buildings were still in position. Dunstall Park station has gone, as have the shops on the corner of Gorsebrook Road (see page 54). On the other hand the ECC is still very much alive.

Wolverhampton gasworks, looking east. Number 14 lock on the Birmingham Canal, which ran through the works, can be seen.

SECTION TWO

Coven

Cross Green bridge, Coven, on the Staffordshire and Worcestershire Canal, photographed in the early twentieth century with local children posed on the towpath. The cottage on the right is the same as the one on page 68.

St Paul's church, Coven, was consecrated in February 1857. Coven was originally in Brewood parish, but Coven Heath was in Bushbury.

Coven Heath chapel, built in the 1880s, was a Church of England chapel in Bushbury parish. It survived the coming of the nearby M54.

Coven Methodist church, Lawn Lane, was built in 1839. The church has not changed since the photograph was taken some fifty years ago.

The War Memorial, Coven, is shown here mounted on a wall opposite the site of the modern parade of shops. It was moved to its present position in the Memorial Hall garden in the 1950s.

The · Ball Inn, Coven.

Near Wolverhampton.

The Ball Inn, Coven Heath, was demolished only in 1981 due to the construction of the M54. The brewery which opened the inn has records dating from 1820, but it may not have been licensed at that time. In White's Directory for 1851 the licensee is listed as Richard Humpage, wheelwright and victualler of the 'Golden Ball', as it was known for some time.

Grange Farm, Coven, which was next door to the Rainbow Inn, photographed in the early twentieth century. Members of the Copeland family are standing at the gate. The house has since been considerably altered, with the front door and windows being moved.

School Lane, Coven. The older part of the school has remained unchanged since this photograph was taken some fifty years ago.

The Rainbow Inn, Coven, photographed in the early twentieth century, showing customers arriving by pony and trap. The Rainbow was rebuilt around 1950.

The Anchor Inn at Cross Green, Coven, in the 1930s. The Staffordshire and Worcestershire Canal is behind the hedge on the right. A few hundred yards north on the canal is a 'winding hole' where boats could turn, and a series of iron rings, set in the towpath, shows where they tied up for the night. On 30 June 1806 T.H.F. Whitgreave, of Moseley Old Hall, recorded in his diary that he was ordering new pottery and tableware, 'to be sent by the navigation directed for T.H.F. Whitgreave near Wolverhampton to be left at the Anchor Inn at Cross Green'. The Anchor was rebuilt in the 1950s.

SECTION THREE
People and Events

The first Bushbury scouts (Staveley-Hill's own) around 1910.

George Thomas Whitgreave
(1787–1863) was the builder of
Moseley Court.

Mrs Amelia Ann Whitgreave
(1790–1848) was the wife of George
Thomas Whitgreave.

The Moreton family at Moseley Hall around 1900. Left to right: Slyn (groom?), R.J. Moreton, Mrs Moreton (behind the pony), J.P. Moreton, George Slaney, Loftus B. Moreton.

Servants of the Moreton family at Moseley Hall around 1912. The photograph shows the butler, Mr Wakefield, with domestic servants, including Alice Evans, née Brazier, who is pictured second from the left, and her life-long friend, Hilda Rushton, second from the right. Mr Wakefield's daughter, Constance, was the first wife of the late Mr Walter Wells, who will be remembered by older residents.

Henry Staveley-Hill (1865–1946) of
Oxley Manor who was MP for this
division of Staffordshire 1905–1918,
Recorder of Banbury 1903–22, a
County Court Judge 1922–8, and
Lieutenant-Colonel commanding
the 2/1 Staffordshire Yeomanry
1916–17.

Mr and Mrs H.J. Winstone at Oxley Manor with their two daughters, Violet and Daisy, in the early years of this century. Mr Winstone was a warden at the parish church for many years.

Mr Leake, coachman at Oxley Manor.

Mr Wellman, coachman to Henry Lovatt, at Low Hill House around 1900.

Gorsebrook House stood on the east side of the Stafford Road, about 100 yards north of the canal bridge, and was demolished in the 1980s. The family may be that of the manager of the Electric Construction Company, who lived at the house after the factory was built in the company's grounds at the turn of the century.

Samuel Clifft and his mother at Fordhouse
Mill Farm around 1900.

Samuel Loyns (1865–1957) farmed at Fordhouse Mill Farm as tenant for Lincoln
College, Oxford, from 1908 until his death in 1957.

The Reverend Percy Ilott, photographed at Bushbury Vicarage, was vicar from 1914–19, when he resigned through ill health.

The Lawrence family at Glebe Cottage in 1906. Joseph Lawrence was sexton/verger at the parish church. The cottage stood on what is now the rectory car park and faced the school. In the 1920s and '30s it was the home of the school caretakers, Mr and Mrs Wood.

Mrs Shinton of Bushbury Hall. This is one of a series of photographs taken either during or just after the First World War, showing her with the horses that were bred at Bushbury Hall Farm.

Miss Tolley of Moseley Court photographed in the field near Berrybrook around 1916. The outbuildings of Underhill Farm can be seen in the distance. One of the original gateposts of the entrance to Moseley Court can still be found in the hedgerow.

Bushbury ex-servicemen photographed at the ECC sports field, Showell Road, in 1919.

The wives of Bushbury ex-servicemen also pictured in 1919 at the ECC sports field.

A float in the Electric Construction Company Carnival, 28 September 1918.

Wolverhampton Auxiliary Fire Service, No. 3 station, Manley & Regulus, Showell Road, photographed in 1941. These were nearly all part-time members with their 'second line out', tender CUK 708, a 1937 Hudson Terraplane conversion. Back row, left to right: Jack Flamank, Tom Ford, A. Nutt, Jack Smith, J. Adams, ? Hatherway. In front of the ladder: A. Bailey, W. Clarke, -?-. In front of the vehicle: -?- , Win Richards, -?- , H.E. Bates, Rose Massey (under ladder). By the pump: Alex Chatwin, Ron Bowker, Len Dodd, ? Winsper, -?-. The chimney on the left is part of Bushbury loco sheds.

Wolverhampton National Fire Service station 3X, Showell Road, Bushbury, photographed in 1944 on the Usam sports field at the corner of Wood Lane and Bee Lane, showing some of the part-time firewomen. Their normal duties were as clerks and telephonists for a few hours on two or three evenings per week. In this photograph they were training to operate a trailer pump in actual fire-fighting work. They were never needed! The people pictured include, back row: Alf Jackson (driver), Alex Chatwin (messenger). Front row: Peggy Jay, Jean Beech, Joan White, Joyce Sutcliffe (peaked cap).

The first Bushbury scouts (Staveley-Hill's own) around 1910.

The first Bushbury scouters, with scoutmaster Jack Hughes, at Shaw Road Mission Room in 1938.

The Church of the Good Shepherd brownies, Low Hill, around 1944. Middle row, left to right: Mary Clark, Joyce Hill, Molly Cotterill, Dorothy Woodall, Mavis Marchant, -?-, -?-. Front row: Ivy Ridgeway, ? Cotterill, -?-, -?-, -?-, Lily Smith.

A VE Day street party in Colley Avenue, Low Hill, in 1945. The children (left to right) are: Mavis Marchant, -?-, Molly (Margaret) Robinson, Colleen Robinson, -?-, -?-. The names of the adults are not known.

Children of Colley Avenue, Low Hill, at the VE Day street party.

Balloon ascent of Henry Coxwell and James Glaisher, 5 September 1862. Filled with coal gas, the balloon took off from the Stafford Road gasworks. It reached a record 37,000 feet and came down near Ludlow.

Launching the Wolverhampton lifeboat, 27 August 1866. Paid for by public subscription, the lifeboat was launched on Bushbury Pool, where this photograph was taken. The *Wolverhampton* was stationed at the Mumbles, near Swansea, and saved many lives in the Bristol Channel until it was lost in a storm in 1883.

The bonfire on Bushbury Hill for Queen Victoria's Diamond Jubilee in 1897.

The Hon. C.S. Rolls in the first Midlands National Aviation Meeting at Dunstall Park, 27 June to 2 July 1910. The plane is the one that Rolls used when he made his cross-Channel flight.

Midlands National Aviation Meeting at Dunstall Park, 27 June to 2 July 1910.

Plane crash at Fordhouses, April 1970. Three people were killed when a twelve-seater, executive aircraft almost demolished a house in Redhurst Drive. The victims were Mrs Nellie Hilton, who lived in the house, the pilot and co-pilot. The plane, belonging to Dowty-Boulton Paul, had been attempting to land at Wolverhampton Airport, Pendeford, which had been under threat of closure for some time. The question of safety had been one of the arguments used in favour of closure, and the crash confirmed the danger of having an airport so close to a built-up area. The airport closed early in 1971.

SECTION FOUR

Industry

Wolverhampton gasworks, from the roof of Stafford Road GWR works. In the days before North Sea gas, Wolverhampton was supplied with gas made at the works on the east side of the Stafford Road. Coal came in by rail, gas went out by pipeline, and the principal by-product, gas-tar, by narrow boat on the Birmingham Canal, which passed through the works. The Goodyear chimney can be seen on the left of the skyline.

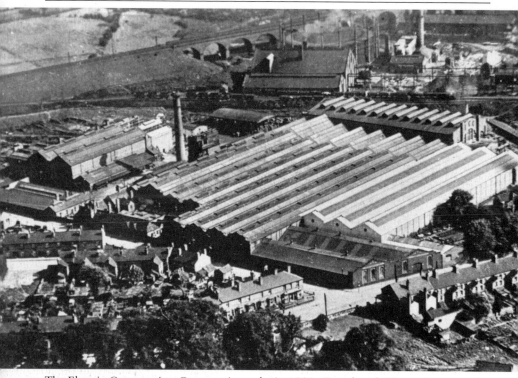

The Electric Construction Company's works in 1921. Gorsebrook House is among the trees on the right. The double-fronted Co-operative store (see page 138) is on the corner, in front of the factory.

The interior of the Electric Construction Company's works. It is difficult both to date the photograph and to identify the manufacturing process. The ECC made a variety of electrical machinery and all types of switchgear during the 1930s, including generators, transformers and motor-control panels.

The construction of Courtauld's, June 1925. Courtauld's, based in Braintree, Essex, had been a textile manufacturer since 1825. It began producing rayon, or 'artificial silk', at Coventry in 1905. The building of a rayon-producing plant in Dunstall, Wolverhampton, was part of the firm's more general expansion into several areas of the country.

Courtauld's works in the 1960s, looking from Newhampton Road towards the racecourse. The works' chimneys were a distinctive feature of the local skyline until their demolition in 1973.

Prince Philip visiting the coning department at Courtauld's in December 1948. Jessie Talbot demonstrates her work.

The Duchess of Kent speaks to Cherry Smith during her visit to Courtauld's in 1968.

Laying the first brick of Goodyear's new factory in 1927. Those pictured include: H.B. Robinson, Wolverhampton Borough engineer, in the light coat on the upper level, Alderman Bantock, with the beard on the platform, A.E. Wood, the mayor, bending over, and F. Warbreck Howell, the town clerk, on the right of the platform.

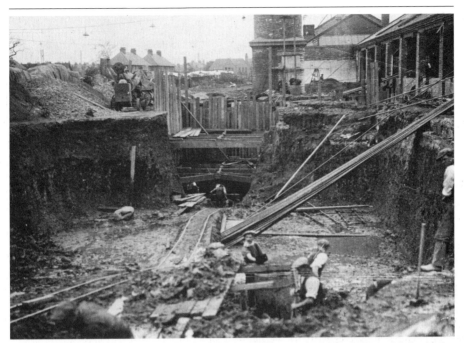

Constructing Goodyear's works in October 1927. Here, the foundations of the boiler house and stack are being excavated.

Tyre builders at Goodyear in 1945. Left to right: George Sibbald, Fred Uzzell, Bernard O'Connell, Jack Darby, Frank Wall, Sidney Downes, Bob Coton, Jim Sadler, George Smith, Frank Wootton, Eric Page, Arthur Edwards, Bill Griffiths, Harry Cooper, Albert Bender. Between them they had more than 200 years of service at Goodyear.

The millionth tyre built at Goodyear, Wolverhampton, in July 1929 was a cause for celebration. The tread was applied by the mayor, A.E. Wood, who is pictured on the left on the platform. Also pictured, left to right: Mr Partridge, the managing director, Mr Sullivan, the company secretary, F.A. Willcock, the deputy mayor, Mr Flannery, the general superintendent.

An aerial view of the Goodyear factory, showing Stafford Road to the left and Bushbury Lane crossing the railway line on the right. The present office block, fronting Stafford Road, was built in 1960 on the field which appears to have an aerial conveyor system or power lines above it. This photograph appeared in the Annual Shareholders Report for 1952.

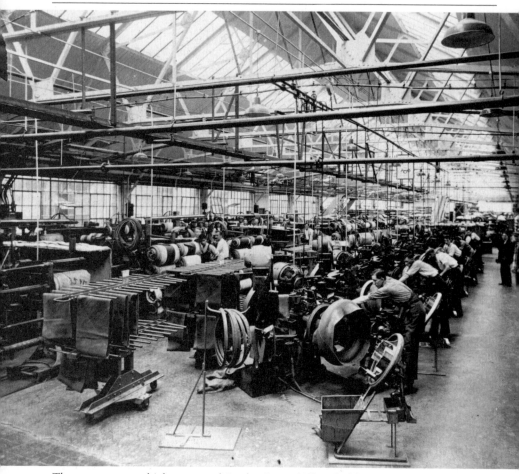

The tyre room, which appeared in the Annual Shareholders Report for 1932, was reproduced in the Goodyear staff magazine, *The Wingfoot Clan*, in December 1947. It shows a row of core-building tyre machines, before the days when conveyors were used, with the bands delivered on 'arm' trucks.

The tyre room at Goodyear, showing the maple floor which was laid shortly after the photograph opposite was taken.

A striking photograph of tyre finishing at Goodyear, probably taken in the 1930s.

Tube-room girls at Goodyear, in March 1930, wearing the factory safety uniform, designed not to be caught in moving machinery. Left to right: Alice Thurston, Gladys Biggs, Florence Baggott, Annie Harrison, Ethel Cope, Ivy Baggott, Irene Howe, Lilian Taylor, Nancy Howe.

The engineering division of Goodyear in 1936, when they won the Inter-Divisional Safety Competition. Front row, left to right: E.G. Worrall, J. Hughes, R. Harley, T. Heritage, H. Millward, J.A. Davies, W. Edwards, H. Mills, W. Leadbetter, A.J. Baston, W. Hartill, F. Nabbs, W.H. Jones, J.E. Southall, A. Birch, T. Haines. Second row: K.M. Walker, W. Smethurst, G.A. Bell, C. Farrington, W.T. Gibson, R. Liversidge, F.A. Steele, W.H. Tyson, Miss N. Gough, Mrs G.E. Newill, J.J. Chase, T. Mulligan, A. Parker, A.B. Westwood, S. Pountney, W.A. Gray, H. Davis. Third row: F. Elwell, J.W.A. Davies, L. Kent, L. Rostance, W.T. Rabone, G. Wigg, G.E. Dalton, W. Llowarch, W. Scott, G. Townend, W. Mansell, H. Williams, F. Dunbar, F. Hill, T. Kent, W. Till, F. Shenton. Fourth row: J. Matheson, G. Tandy, A. Terry, W.H. Jones, F. Lilly, J. Stainton, M.M. Blair, C. Mounsey, S.T. Hucker, A. Taylor, W. Watson, W. Knott, W.T. Wood, W. Hall, T. Hickin. Back row: R. Grove, A. Farmer, C. Woodford, J. Lloyd, H. Colley, N. Reece, J. Marsh, A. Carter, K. Arrowsmith, F. Thorn, A. Cope, E.E. Griffiths, A. White, F. Wright, A. Broatch, J. Brabbins, M. Hereward, B. Collins, R. Hadley, S.B. Brown.

The Goodyear Fire Brigade in the 1950s. Standing, left to right: Firemen France, Forde, Peate, Yates, Duke, Shergold, Clarke, Tapper, Webb, Haynes, Langford, Leading Fireman Hughes, Firemen Humphreys, Rabone, Perry, Stamp, Bancroft, Evans, Wright, Stibbs, Butler, Middleton, Haddock, Smith. Seated: Senior Fireman Smith, Leading Fireman Heritage, K.M. Waker, Second Officer Whatmore, H.L. Ginaven, Commanding Officer Webb, Miss K.M. Rostance, Senior Officer Best, Leading Fireman Dawes, Senior Fireman Marriott.

The Goodyear Police in 1928. Standing, left to right: F. Cashmere, B. Lee, H. Wobd, T. White, W. Law, W. Webb. Seated: F. Sheldon, J. Manning, J.B. Corbett.

Goodyear Home Guard gun team during the Second World War. Standing, left to right: F. Rees, E. Rogers, J.H. Thompson, W.H. Chitty, J. Payne, A. Wainwright. Seated: L. Whitehouse, E. Shelton, F. Purchase.

Goodyear calender room workers in April 1930. Back row, left to right: A. Spragg, T. Ronaldson, G. Thomas, J. Quinton, E. Fellows, J. Duke, E. Dolloway, N. Hinks, C. Van Dyke, R. Thomas. Front row: R. Clarke, P. Whyton, W. Pritchard, J. Cole, J. Billau, S. Brice, R. Kirby, J. Millward, L. Cording, A. Potter.

Goodyear swimming club's first gala at Heath Town Baths in 1937. As well as the usual races, the gala included diving for plates on the bottom of the pool, an obstacle race, and a boat race.

SECTION FIVE

Transport

Aldersley Junction, showing the first lock leading into the Birmingham Canal from the Staffordshire and Worcestershire Canal. In the 1930s as many as twenty working narrow boats would be tied up here at weekends. Today the traffic is mainly from pleasure craft. The lock-keeper's cottage was demolished in the 1960s.

Bushbury Tram Terminus, Stafford Road. This service started in 1905 and was part of the Lorain System introduced into Wolverhampton in 1902. Bushbury Lane lies behind the tram.

Bushbury Tram Terminus, Oxley Bank. The tram is at the end of the line at the bottom of Bushbury Lane. On the left is the entrance to Oxley House.

Laying the tramlines to Bushbury in Stafford Road, 1903. This section of the road ran between the high walls of the GWR works, which were on both sides of it. Part of the footbridge which connected the two parts of the works can be seen above the man on the left.

Stafford Road works. This group of engine drivers was photographed in the 1920s and includes Mr A. Attfield, at the rear of the cab, Mr A. Davis and Jimmy Powell in the back row, Sid Clapham, Bill Lines, Bill Hicken and Joe Chick in the middle row, and Alf Knowles in the front row.

Interior of the Stafford Road works in 1963, showing a 56XX class 0–6–2T locomotive nearing the end of a major overhaul. Behind it is an 84XX class 0–6–0PT still stripped of its tanks.

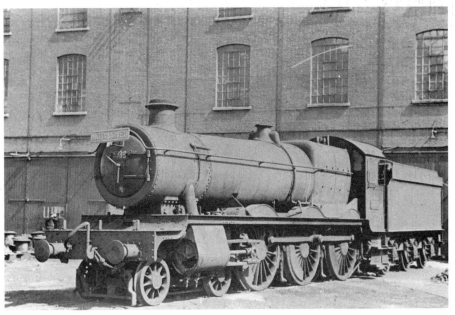

Stationary boiler at the Stafford Road works. The ex-5938, *Stanley Hall*, which was withdrawn, redundant and with a broken cylinder, stands outside the erecting shop in 1963. The large wooden doors give access to the repair roads inside.

Stafford Road railway works pictured on Easter Monday 1949, doubtless an unusually quiet scene. In 1959 the works became a repair depot only, and finally closed completely in February 1964.

Stafford Road railway works' fire brigade around 1948.

Drivers' instruction class, at the Stafford Road works, studying the workings of a side-valve in the 1920s. On the wall behind is a diagram of a piston valve. Drivers attended these lessons in their own time, without pay.

Oxley sidings in 1897, showing the expansion which had taken place that year. The sidings were on the Great Western network and the wagons are being pulled by an 0–6–0 tender engine.

Oxley sidings at a later date, showing open-cabbed saddle tanks built at the Stafford Road works.

Oxley Middle signal box in the 1950s. The signalman is Albert Ellis.

Shunters at Oxley in the 1950s.

Oxley shed, which was opened in 1908 and demolished in 1968. The engines grouped around one of its two turntables include a 4700 class, a Hall 4900 class, and a 2301 Dean class.

Oxley viaduct, a blue-grey brick structure of thirteen arches, marked the furthest point north reached by the GWR broad gauge system. It was used as a shunting neck for trains to reverse up to Victoria Basin. The train crossing the viaduct is a Shrewsbury to Birkenhead express.

Bushbury shed on the London and North Western Railway system (later the London and Midland) in 1959. The shed dates from the late 1850s and has expanded over the years. In the background is the mechanized, ash handling plant installed in the 1930s. The locomotive at the front is one of the Staniers Black 5s designed in the 1930s. Behind it is one of the LNW's most successful designs, the 0–8–0 goods locomotive, designed early in the century and still working in the 1960s at the end of the steam era.

SECTION SIX

Church and School

Bushbury churchyard, showing the large white memorial erected by parishioners to their vicar, William Lister, who died in 1864, and his wife Catherine. The Staveley-Hill family grave and memorial is on the right.

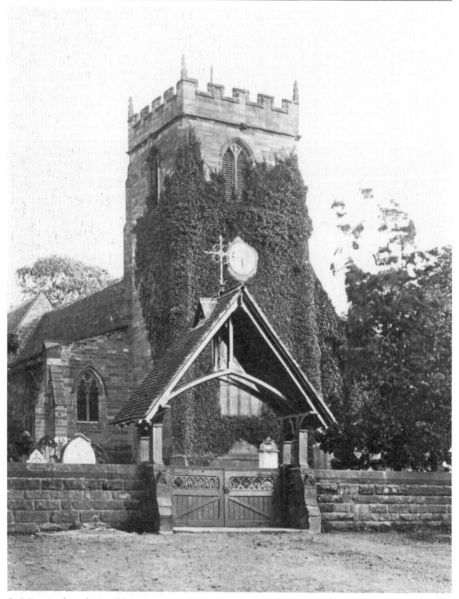

St Mary's church, Bushbury, in 1890, showing the lych-gate donated by Miss Theodosia Hinckes in 1863. The original church dates from Saxon times with the oldest remaining part, the chancel, dating from around 1350. The church was largely rebuilt in the early 1830s, but twenty years later it was decided that the new parts were 'a thing too monstrous to be longer borne' and it was redesigned by Edward Banks, a Wolverhampton architect. The subsequent work resulted in the church looking very much as it is today. The tower was one part of this reconstruction and remained covered in creeper until the early years of the twentieth century.

The War Memorial, St Mary's church, which was put up in the 1920s. The list of names was extended after the Second World War.

Interior of St Mary's, Bushbury, in the 1920s. The pews, which were installed after the rebuilding in 1853, are still in position. The oil lamps were replaced with electric lighting around 1932.

Bushbury church choir pictured around 1930. The vicar, the Revd J.T. Crathorne, is in the centre of the second row.

Bushbury Sunday School Festival in 1955. The old schoolhouse, which was used by the headmaster until the 1920s, can be clearly seen. It was demolished shortly after the photograph was taken.

The temporary iron church, Low Hill, which was the only church on the estate when it was built in 1927 by the Wesleyans. The cost, including furnishing, was £342.

Laying the foundation stone of Low Hill Methodist church on Michaelmas Day 1928. The stone was laid by the mayor, Councillor A.E. Wood, pictured to the right of the stone. Other people present included Councillor Joseph Clark (middle of the front row, to the mayor's right) and representatives of the Trinity circuit, and Primitive and United Methodist circuits.

Low Hill Wesleyan Methodist church early in the 1930s. The church was opened in 1929 and cost £7,750, a contrast to the temporary iron church which continued to be used as a Sunday school for some years.

Bushbury Methodist church, Shaw Road, was built in the 1880s and was the first Protestant, Non-Conformist church in Bushbury, catering mainly for the railway employees who moved into the area in the 1870s and '80s. It was demolished in the 1980s shortly after this photograph was taken.

Bushbury Old Council School in 1908. The school marathon team was photographed with the headmaster, Francis Burton, who served from 1876 until 1915. Looking at their ages it seems unlikely that the team competed in a marathon of twenty-six miles, as we know it today.

Bushbury Old Council School in the early 1920s. The headmaster, Mr Pidgeon, is pictured with senior girls and boys and another teacher whose name is not known. At this time the school was not in Wolverhampton Borough and there was no senior school nearby. Pupils stayed from the ages of five to fourteen. The school was established in 1835 by Miss Theodosia Hinckes. It was a church school and was built close to the lych-gate. The original building included a master's house, now demolished, and the rooms on the north side of the present building, now in use as a nursery school and library.

Staff of Bushbury Old Council School around 1930. Back row, left to right: Mr Bates, Miss Jones (whom he later married), Miss Elwell, Mr Ely. Seated: Miss Austin, Miss Phillips, Mr Pidgeon (headmaster), Mrs Mason, Miss Lowenthal.

Pupils at Bushbury Old Council School around 1928. Fourth row from front, second from right: Joan Bachelor. Third row, fourth from left: Ivy Fowler. Fifth from right: Muriel Chatwin. First right: Roy Darlington. Second row, third from left: Ivor Darlington.

Bushbury Old Council School, with Mr Bates and his class, around 1929.

Staff of Bushbury Old Council School around 1940. Back row, left to right: -?-, Mrs Mason, Miss Phillips, Mrs Cattermole. Seated: -?-, Mr R.S. Ruston (headmaster), Miss Hemingway. Seated on the ground: Miss Bott, Miss Mayhew.

Bushbury Old Council School in the 1930s, when the north side of Bushbury Lane was still undeveloped. The road opposite the school is the Old School Lane and not Collingwood Road. The bus-stop was the terminus of the number 33 bus route, and the building on the extreme left is Church Farm.

Bushbury Lane School between 1901 and 1904. The original Bushbury Lane School was built by Mr and Mrs Staveley-Hill on the corner of Bushbury Lane and the present Ripon Road. It was known as the 'Concrete' school and was replaced in 1909 by a larger building in Ripon Road, also called Bushbury Lane School and now Oxley Primary School. The 'Concrete' school was designed to be used as both school and chapel, and continued in use as a hall after 1909. It finished its life as a store for Goodyear and was demolished in the 1960s.

Bushbury Lane School around 1930. The children all have slates in front of them for writing on, rather than paper.

Pupils at Bushbury Lane School in 1927. Back row, left to right: H. Onions, A. Loons, K. Smith, J. Stirlaker. Middle row: F. Paget, D. Brassington, -?-, Lorna Birch, F. Pillinger, N. Parkes. Front row: Horace Rose, Tony Whittle, ? Stevens.

Bushbury Hill Junior School around 1929. This class was being held in one of the temporary huts used before the present school was built. The children are pictured with their harvest gifts.

Bushbury Hill School football team in 1939. The teacher is Mr Norman Beddoes.

Old Fallings Junior School football team in 1936.

Old Fallings Junior School cricket team in 1936. Back row, second from left: Eric Marchant. Front row, third from left: Billy Crooks(?), who later played football for England.

Whitgreave School pupils in 1932. The boy third from the left was Eric Marchant. The school was formerly known as Twelfth Avenue School and occupied 'temporary' wooden premises for forty years in what is now Whitgreave Avenue (formerly Twelfth Avenue). The present school was built in Goodyear Avenue in the 1970s.

SECTION SEVEN

Shops and Services

The lodge to Oxley House stood on the west side of Stafford Road, opposite the old end of Bushbury Lane at the bottom of the drive to Oxley House. From the 1930s it was Messrs Mascall's Wet and Fried fish shop. It was demolished when this part of the road became a dual carriageway, and the entrance to Oxley House re-routed via South Street.

The general store in Jones Road around 1910. The store was run by Miss Helen Aulton.

Showell Circus shops around 1930. The shops were planned when the Low Hill estate was designed; in fact the plans included space for two rows but the other shops came at a later date. Left to right: Miss Morris, children's clothes and drapery; Miss O'Shea, post office; Marriot, grocer; Henry Hill, butcher; Walter Jones, greengrocer; the Co-operative store; Rogers, tobacco and sweets; Broatch, grocer; Warrilow, ironmonger, who had facilities for recharging lead/acid batteries for early radios; Cullwick, bread, cakes, home-made fish and meat pastes.

Bushbury's first Co-operative shop in the 1920s. It stood on the east side of Stafford Road at the junction with Showell Road (see page 92). The bay windows were later replaced by a proper shop front.

Interior of Oxley Co-operative store in November 1966.

Opening of Oxley Co-operative supermarket, 10 November 1966. The shop was opened by 'Batman', and advertised a car park at the rear and handy buses. The building, fronting the Stafford Road, is still there.

Shops at Stafford Road, Oxley, on the corner of Church Road. The variety of styles suggests that these shops were not all purpose-built; the fruit stores and butchers appear to be in a converted house.

Three Tuns Parade, Stafford Road, which was built in the 1930s to serve the growing population in the Marsh Lane area. It took its name from the nearby public house.

Shops at Oxley in 1926. These shops are in Stafford Road, close to the junction with Church Road. The garage stands on the site of a late eighteenth-century blacksmith's shop.

Collingwood Road shopping parade was built in the 1950s to serve the new estate which had been built opposite the church.

Park Lane clinic was built in the early 1930s to serve the people on the Low Hill estate.

Low Hill Community Hall opened in 1937. The following year it was used as a centre for the issue of gas masks.

Low Hill Library, which was originally Bushbury Branch Library, opened in 1930. As with the other community buildings it is situated in Showell Circus, the focal point of the estate as it was planned. Older residents remember the popularity of the children's library at this time; a teacher's signature was needed on the membership application. The interior view, while recognizable, shows several changes. The central desk was of a very similar design to that in the Central Library reference department, and to other early branches such as Heath Town and Bilston.

Bushbury Branch Library, Oxley, was opened in 1950 on the corner of Stafford Road and Lymer Road. Previously people had to use a branch library in Elston Hall School, which only opened one night a week. The new library was open six days a week and had a children's section and reading room. The photograph dates from the 1950s and shows B. Williams, a library assistant.

Oxley Library was built on the site of the old Rakegate Farm in Probert Road to replace Bushbury Branch Library in the late 1950s. The library continued to be known by its old name until around 1976. The photograph was taken in 1961.

Leisure

Courtauld's works Queen at her enthronement during the annual Sports Day in 1935. The Queen, Miss G. Waterfall, was crowned by Miss E. Gaskin.

The main entrance to Dunstall Park Racecourse. Wolverhampton Racecourse was originally in the town centre, where the West Park is now; Dunstall Park was opened in 1888. During the Second World War the offices and stables were used by the local fire service and later, in NFS days, as a training school. There was a battery of anti-aircraft rockets stationed on the racecourse.

Gordon Richards wins his one-hundredth race in the Bushbury Selling Handicap at Dunstall Park on 13 October 1925.

Dunstall Park Racecourse on 20 August 1923. The jockey is Steve Donoghue. In the background a steam train is making its way across Oxley viaduct.

elling Handicap. 15 Runners.   Photo by Arcade Studio,

e Hundredth Success.   Wolverhampton

Aerial view of Dunstall Park Racecourse and Aldersley Athletics Stadium taken in 1959. The stadium lies to the left of the racecourse with the Staffordshire and Worcestershire Canal in between. The Birmingham Canal can be seen along the top of the racecourse beneath the railway sidings, and the Oxley viaduct stands out clearly. The two canals meet at Autherley Junction, which is just off this view to the left. The railway line that led to Wimbourne, now the Valley Park Linear Walkway, can be seen across the left-hand corner of the stadium, and Courtauld's factory is to the right of the racecourse.

The official opening of Aldersley Stadium took place on 9 June 1956 and was performed by Jack Hawkins, the actor, who was in Wolverhampton filming *Man in the Sky*, part of which was filmed at Wolverhampton Airport, Pendeford. The opening meeting was an inter-counties match between the Midland Counties AAA, Northern Counties AAA and Southern Counties AAA. The first event was a 500-yard cycle handicap, and other events included a long jump match, a hop, step and jump match, and a 120-yard hurdles match. There was an interval during which the finish of the Rhyl to Wolverhampton Cycle Road Race took place.

The opening of St Christopher's Park and Training Ground in Fifth Avenue, Low Hill, was performed on 7 July 1951 by Major-General B.K. Young, director general of the Royal Society for the Prevention of Accidents. It was known locally as the 'Penny Bike Park' and was later converted for use as a track for BMX cycles. In the last six years it has been transformed into an award-winning wildlife park.

A policeman gives instruction on procedure at a pedestrian crossing at St Christopher's training ground.

The traffic training ground, St Christopher's Park, on the opening day. The scheme was designed to teach children road safety while they played, and the training ground was laid out as a miniature road system. Children were able to hire cycles for a small fee and ride around the roads. Posters gave information from the *Highway Code* and police visited on occasions to give advice. The motor bus in the photograph was only there for the opening day. A film was made at the park for training purposes.

Dunstall cinema, which stood opposite the end of Bushbury Lane on the Stafford Road, opened in November 1934, becoming the Dunstall Odeon two years later. It closed as a cinema in 1960 and stood empty until it re-opened as a bingo hall in 1962. It became part of the Hutchinson Group (Surewin Bingo) in 1971 and remained with them until it closed in September 1981. The building was demolished in November that year when road widening took place.

Bushbury Baths in Sandy Lane were first planned in 1955 and finally opened in December 1966. The building, designed by the Borough architect, Mr A. Chapman, was controversial although it won a commendation in the Civic Trust Awards in 1969.

The Gate Inn stood on the west side of Stafford Road between Wobaston Lane and Coven Heath. It is not known when it was built, but an unnamed beer-house stood on the site early in the nineteenth century. The photograph dates from around 1930; the building was demolished only seven years later when the dual carriageway was constructed.

The Butler's Arms, a mix of mock Dutch and Victoriana, was built in 1937 when Kempthorne Avenue was extended from Low Hill Crescent to Bushbury Lane. There was a wide selection of rooms beside the large public bar, including a lounge and several smoke-rooms and snugs. It was demolished a few years ago and the site redeveloped for a supermarket.

The Bushbury Arms, in Showell Circus, was built in the 1920s to cater for the new Low Hill estate. There was some controversy surrounding the sale of land to the Council by the Low Hill-Bushbury Estate Company, when it emerged that two central plots had been withheld and sold directly to Atkinson's brewery along with a monopoly on the sale of beer, spirits etc. The brewery was eventually obliged to sell the land to the Council. The photograph shows the pub decorated for the coronation celebrations in 1953.

The Three Tuns Inn, on the Stafford Road, is a relatively recent building, dating back to around 1930, although there had been an inn on the site for at least 200 years. In the 1780s it was bought, with an adjoining farm, by Erasmus Darwin, the poet, philosopher and scientist. He was a shareholder in the Staffordshire and Worcestershire Canal Company, and was probably interested in the land, which extended down Marsh Lane to the canal. The innkeeper at the time, William Buxton, was his tenant. In the 1820s there was a toll-gate outside the inn.

The opening of the Staffordshire Volunteer, on 23 July 1957, by Mrs R.F. Ilsley, mayor of Wolverhampton. This new public house was built at the same time as the Northicote estate.

The Oxley Arms was built in the nineteenth century and stood in Bushbury Lane until it was demolished earlier this year. It was known locally as 'The Manor' and was a 'North Western' pub, frequented generally by people employed by that railway company, and rarely by employees of the Great Western Railway Company. It had a function room upstairs for club meetings such as the 'Loyal Caledonian Corks Friendly Society', and there was a fair-sized garden outside for parents and children. There was also a bowling green with a very strong Crown Green Bowls team in the 1930s.

The Locomotive Inn, which stood at Five Ways on Stafford Road. The name would appear to have some connection with the nearby GWR works whose employees were, no doubt, its main customers. The licensee, pictured in the 1920s, was Bert Adey who later moved to be landlord of the Pear Tree Inn on Cannock Road and was famous for staging outdoor boxing tournaments.

Acknowledgements

All the photographs in this book are in the collection of Wolverhampton Libraries, and the authors are most grateful to all those who have donated photographs to the collection, either in the past or specifically for this book, and given permission for their use.

We wish to acknowledge the following people, in particular, for help in donating photographs or providing information: John Beswick, Jim Boulton, Mr G.J. Brown, David Wilkinson Cocking, Mr M.G. Davies, headmaster of Northicote School, Mr P. Eisenhofer, *Express and Star* Newspaper, Mr Gareth Jones, Ms Muriel Lines, Mr McNish, Mrs Pat Malone, Mr A. Robbins, Mr W. Rowney, Staffordshire Record Office, Mr A. Whittle, Ned Williams.

Alex Chatwin would like to personally acknowledge the following people who have given or loaned him photographs over the years: Mr J. Alson, Mrs M. Bates, Miss D.B. Bowker, Mrs F. Edwards, Mr R. Fellows, Mrs B. Pucknall, Mrs J. Rackham, Miss F. Varty.